BIAS DETECTIVES

How we caught the computer being unfair.

By:

David King

Web: www.ingenepublishers.com

Printed in the United Kingdom.

Marketed & Distributed by

Ingene Publications,

63 Fernhead Road Maida Vale, W9, London

Note to Readers

Dear Reader,

This is a story about four friends, a youth club, and a list on a wall that didn't feel quite right. It's also a story about computers, but not the kind that just play games or show videos. These are computers that help adults make big decisions about people's lives.

As you read, you'll see that the "bad guy" here is not a single person or even a single machine. The real problem is what happens when we stop asking questions and just trust a system because it looks clever or official. Amira, Jay, Tomas and Asha discover that fairness isn't automatic, you have to build it on purpose, test it, and fix it when it goes wrong.

You do not need to be a "tech genius" to understand this book. If you've ever looked at a rule and thought, "That doesn't seem fair," you already think like a Bias Detective. The maths and computer science in this story are real ideas, but they are told in a way that anyone can follow.

As you turn the pages, I hope you start to notice patterns in the world around you who gets chosen, who gets left out, and what questions nobody seems to be asking. You don't have to accept those patterns as if they can't change. You are allowed to say, "Show me how this works." You are allowed to say, "We can build this better."

Most of all, I hope this book convinces you of one simple thing: the future of AI doesn't only belong to programmers and big companies. It also belongs to young people who care about justice, community and each other. People like you.

Welcome to the BIAS Detectives.

— David King

Table of Contents

Acknowledgements

Writing *The Bias Detectives* has been a team effort, just like the club in the story.

First, thank you to the young people students, coders, gamers, readers and activists who shared their questions and frustrations about "fairness" in school systems, exams, social media and everyday life. Your stories helped shape Amira, Jay, Tomas and Asha, and reminded me that curiosity and courage are already alive in classrooms and youth clubs everywhere.

I am deeply grateful to colleagues and fellow researchers working on algorithmic bias and AI ethics, whose conversations and critiques sharpened the ideas in this book. You know who you are; thank you for challenging easy answers and insisting that real people's lives always come first.

Thank you to the librarians, teachers and youth workers who open their doors after hours, fix broken laptops, print out forms, and quietly make sure no one is left behind. The Eastside Youth Centre is fictional, but it is inspired by places you keep alive every day.

To my editor and publishing team at Ingene Publishers, thank you for believing that children can handle complex questions and that they deserve stories that respect their intelligence.

To my family and friends, for patience, encouragement and endless conversations about "just one more chapter." And finally, to every reader who picks up this book: thank you for giving these characters your time and attention. I hope they inspire you to ask better questions, and maybe to start your own version of the AI Builders Club.

CHAPTER 1

The List on the Wall

The Eastside Youth Centre smelled like old trainers, microwave popcorn, and possibility.

That was how Amira Rahman always described it to people who'd never been. They usually looked at her like she was strange, but she didn't mind. She'd learned a long time ago that most people skipped the details. Amira never did.

It was a Tuesday in October, the kind of grey afternoon that made East London look like it was filmed through a foggy lens, and Amira arrived at the centre fourteen minutes early as she always did. She liked the quiet before it filled up. She liked to observe how a room changed when people walked into it.

She pulled her notebook from under her arm dark blue, battered at the corners, covered in no stickers whatsoever, because stickers were distracting and settled into her usual chair near the window.

That was when she noticed the board.

A bright yellow sheet of paper had been pinned to the corkboard by the entrance, surrounded by the usual clutter of flyers for football trials and homework club. But this one had a border printed in bold black and a heading that read:

COMMUNITY FUTURES GRANT, SUCCESSFUL APPLICANTS

And below it, a list of names.

Amira stood, crossed the room in twelve steps (she counted without meaning to), and read the list carefully.

Fifteen youth projects had applied for the Community Futures Grant a £5,000 award given by a local charitable trust to fund youth initiatives across the borough. The grant had been running for six years. Amira knew this because she'd looked it up when Mrs Okafor, the centre manager, had announced last month that they were applying.

The Eastside Digital Explorers Club had applied. They wanted funding to buy equipment proper laptops, not the ancient machines in the back room that wheezed when you opened more than two tabs and to run coding workshops for young people in the area. Amira had helped write the application herself.

She ran her finger down the list.

The Eastside Digital Explorers Club was not on it.

She read it again. Slower this time.

Still not on it.

"They posted it already?"

The voice came from behind her, loud and slightly out of breath.

Jayden Clarke Jay, to everyone who knew him, arrived the way he always did: slightly late, slightly rumpled, laptop bag swinging from one shoulder, grinning before he'd even assessed the situation. He was twelve, shorter than Amira by about four centimetres, and he had the kind of energy that made people feel like something was about to happen.

His laptop bag was covered in stickers. Amira had once counted twenty-seven.

"They posted it," Amira confirmed, stepping aside so he could see.

Jay leaned in, scanning the list with the speed of someone who was used to processing information fast he'd told her once that reading felt like scrolling, and she'd understood exactly what he meant.

His grin faded.

"We're not on it."

"No."

"That's" He stopped. Frowned. "Okay. That's weird."

By the time Tomas Nowak arrived, a small group had gathered near the board.

Tomas was fourteen and had the particular talent of making any room feel like a negotiation was about to happen. He was the tallest of the four of them, wore a dark bomber jacket regardless of the weather, and carried himself with the relaxed confidence of someone who'd sat in enough meetings with adults to stop being impressed by them.

He walked in, assessed the room in about three seconds, and came straight over.

"The grant list?" he said, not even looking at the board, just reading the group's faces.

"We didn't get it," Jay said.

Tomas looked at the list. His expression didn't shift dramatically. He just raised one eyebrow the slight, measured kind and said, "Who did?"

They read through the successful projects together.

There were eight winners listed:

Riverside Dance Academy Expansion
Millbrook Football Skills Programme
Heritage Cooking Club
West Side Chess & Debate Society
Riverside Arts Studio
North End Podcast Club
Millbrook Film Workshop
Riverside Junior Entrepreneurs Circle

Amira was quiet for a moment, notebook now open, pen moving.

"Notice anything?" Amira said, not looking up from her notebook.

Jay leaned over. "They're all... the same kind of project?"

"Look at the names," Amira said.

Jay looked. Tomas looked. They read the names again.

"Riverside," Jay said slowly. "Millbrook. Riverside. West Side. Riverside again. North End. Millbrook. Riverside."

"Three are from Riverside," Tomas said. "Two from Millbrook."

"And none," said Amira, "from Eastside."

There was a short pause.

"That could just be coincidence," Tomas said. He wasn't dismissing it he was testing it, the way he always tested things before committing to them.

"It could be," Amira agreed. "But it's a pattern. And patterns are worth investigating."

That was when Asha Patel arrived.

Asha was eleven and the youngest of the group by several months, which she treated as entirely irrelevant. She came through the door at a pace that was just slightly faster than a walk, backpack bouncing, keychains jangling, and she was already talking.

"I saw it from outside," she announced. "The list. We didn't get it. I could see your faces through the window and I knew immediately. What's the plan?"

Jay laughed despite himself. "We literally just found out."

"Okay, but what do we think happened?" Asha said, reaching into her backpack front pocket and pulling out a pad of sticky notes yellow, a thick stack of them.

"We're not sure yet," Amira said. "But I think the selection process needs looking at."

"The grant website said the decision was made using their new automated assessment tool," Tomas said. He'd been on his phone since the conversation started, quietly gathering information. "It's an AI scoring system. They introduced it this year to make the process more consistent."

Everyone looked at him.

"I read the trustees' update from September," he said, sliding his phone back into his jacket pocket. "It was in the newsletter."

"Nobody reads the newsletter," Jay said.

"I read the newsletter."

They found a table in the corner the one with the wonky leg that everyone avoided, which meant they were usually left alone and sat down.

Asha had already started writing on her sticky notes: *Why didn't we get it? AI tool what does that mean? Is it fair?* She stuck them to the edge of the table in a row.

"So," Jay said, opening his laptop the screen casting that familiar blue glow across his face "they used an AI to decide who got the grant."

"To *help* decide," Tomas corrected. "Or at least that's what they'd say."

"What's the difference?" Asha asked.

"That," said Amira, "is exactly the right question."

Jay pulled up the Community Futures Grant website and turned the laptop so they could all see. There was a brief paragraph under a tab labelled *Our Process*:

"This year, initial applications are assessed using an AI-assisted scoring tool that evaluates each proposal against our established criteria. Scores are reviewed by our panel before final decisions are made."

"Established criteria," Amira said, reading carefully. "What criteria?"

"It doesn't say," Jay said.

"So we don't know what it was scoring on."

"No."

"Or what data it was trained on," Jay added. His eyes had gone slightly distant, the way they did when he was thinking rather than talking. "AI tools machine learning systems they learn from past examples. Whatever the grant process looked like *before*, that's what the AI probably learned from."

"Meaning?" Asha asked.

"Meaning if the old system had certain patterns in it who got funded, who didn't the AI might have picked those up and repeated them."

The table was quiet for a moment.

"We need to know how many years this grant has run," Amira said.

"Six," said Tomas.

"And whether they published the results each year."

"Some years," Tomas said. "I've seen at least three years listed on the archive section."

"Then that's where we start." Amira looked at each of them in turn. Her voice was steady, measured. Not angry. Determined. "We don't know yet whether anything went wrong. Maybe we didn't score well for entirely fair reasons. But we have a right to understand the process. And if the process has a flaw in it if the AI learned something it shouldn't have then it's not just our project that's affected."

"It's everyone who applied from areas like ours," Asha said quietly.

She wrote on a new sticky note *everyone affected?* And pressed it firmly to the table.

"Exactly," said Amira.

Mrs Okafor stopped by the table as she was crossing the room, carrying a folder and a mug of tea.

She was the centre manager broad, warm, no-nonsense, with reading glasses she was always misplacing and a direct way of speaking that Amira respected.

"I saw you lot huddled. Everything alright?"

"We were looking at the grant results," Tomas said.

Mrs Okafor's expression shifted slightly. "Yes. Disappointing. I'm going to write to the trust and ask for feedback."

"Can we help?" Amira asked.

Mrs Okafor looked at her really looked, the way adults rarely did.

"What did you have in mind?"

"We want to look at the data," Amira said. "Past winners. The scoring criteria. How the AI tool works. We think there might be a pattern worth understanding."

Mrs Okafor was quiet for a moment. Then she said, "I'd need to see what you find before anything goes anywhere official."

"Of course," Amira said.

"Then yes. You can help."

Jay typed the first search into his browser: *Community Futures Grant past winners 2019 2020 2021.*

Amira opened to a fresh page in her notebook and wrote at the top, pressing hard enough to leave an indent:

What did the AI learn, and from what?

Asha stuck a final note to the corner of her laptop screen where she'd always see it:

Fair for who?

And Tomas leaned back in his chair, arms folded, looking at the board across the room, the yellow list, the names that were there, and the one that wasn't.

"Right," he said quietly. "Let's figure this out."

CHAPTER 2

How Machines Learn

The next afternoon, Jay arrived first.

This was unusual enough that Amira noted it in her notebook without meaning to, *Jay: early. First time.* and then crossed it out because it wasn't relevant to their investigation. Then she uncrossed it because actually, it probably said something about how much this mattered to him.

He'd pushed two tables together in the corner, the wonky one and a slightly more stable one beside it, and had his laptop open, a second browser window running on Mrs Okafor's old desktop computer that she'd agreed to let them use, and three hand-drawn diagrams spread across the table in marker on large sheets of paper.

"You've been busy," Tomas said, arriving next and studying the sheets.

"I couldn't sleep," Jay said, without embarrassment. "I kept thinking about training data."

When Asha arrived and settled in, sticky notes ready, and Amira had her notebook open, Jay began.

"Okay," he said, capping his marker. "I'm going to explain how machine learning works. And I'm going to do it without making it boring, because it's actually not boring at all."

"Noted," said Tomas.

"So. Imagine you want to teach a computer to recognise cats."

Asha raised her hand. "I love this already."

"You don't programme it with a list of rules, *has whiskers, has four legs, makes a suspicious noise at 3am.* That's the old way. Instead, you show it thousands and thousands of pictures of cats. And thousands of pictures of things that are *not* cats. And you let it figure out the pattern itself."

"How does it figure it out?" Amira asked.

"It makes a guess, checks if it's right, adjusts, guesses again. Over and over. Millions of times. Until it gets really good at recognising the pattern." Jay tapped the funnel diagram. "The stuff you feed into the funnel, all those example pictures, that's called training data. The pattern it learns is called the model."

"Right," said Amira slowly. "So whatever is in the training data, the AI learns from that."

"Exactly."

"Including any mistakes in it."

"Yes."

"Or any biases."

Jay pointed at her. "That's the thing. If the examples you feed it already have a pattern of unfairness in them, if, say, in all your example photos, cats are always shown indoors and dogs are always shown outdoors, the AI might accidentally learn that *location* is part of what makes something a cat. Even though it isn't."

"That's not just an accident," Tomas said. "That's the AI learning the wrong lesson from real data."

"Right. And it won't tell you that's what it learned. It'll just... act on it."

There was a pause while everyone absorbed this.

Asha stuck a note to the table: *AI learns from examples. Bad examples = bad learning.*

"So let's say," Amira said carefully, "that for six years, the Community Futures Grant was given to certain kinds of projects from certain parts of the borough. And those results were used as the training data for the new AI scoring tool."

"Then the AI would learn," Jay said, "that projects like those, from those areas, are the 'right' kind of project to fund."

"Even if the only reason they were funded was historical luck, or who knew who, or which areas had better support writing applications."

"Even then. The AI doesn't know *why* something was funded. It just sees that it was. And it learns to repeat the pattern."

"Let's test it," Jay said. He turned to the desktop screen. "I built a small simulation last night."

"You built a simulation," Tomas repeated.

"It's basic. But it works."

On the screen was a simple programme, blocks of colour representing fictional grant applicants, organised into three imaginary areas he'd called Red Zone, Blue Zone, and Green Zone. The simulation would score them based on a set of historical results Jay had invented, weighted toward Blue Zone.

"Watch what happens," Jay said, and ran it.

The results appeared almost instantly. Blue Zone projects filled the top scores. A few Green Zone. Red Zone sat clustered near the bottom, even though Jay had deliberately made their project descriptions just as strong.

"I made all the projects equally good," Jay said. "Same quality descriptions, same community need scores, same everything. But because the historical data I fed it had Blue Zone winning more often, the model learned that Blue Zone projects are better."

"That's—" Asha started.

"Unfair," Amira said.

"Systematically unfair," Tomas said. "Because it's not random. It will keep happening every time the tool is used."

Asha was writing furiously on sticky notes.

The AI isn't mean. It just learned wrong.
But the result is still unfair.
Who is responsible?

She lined them up along the table edge, read them in order, then looked up.

"If the AI isn't doing it on purpose," she said, "does that mean nobody is responsible?"

The question sat in the air.

"That's what some people would say," Tomas said carefully. "That it's just the tool. That nobody decided to be unfair."

"But somebody decided to use the tool," Amira said. "Somebody decided what data to train it on. Somebody decided to trust its results." She looked at her notebook. "Decisions were made. Even if they didn't feel like decisions at the time."

Jay nodded slowly. "That's what I was thinking about last night. You can create harm without ever choosing to. But once you *know*, once someone shows you, then you can't call it an accident anymore."

Mrs Okafor appeared at the table's edge with two packets of biscuits, which she set down without ceremony.

"Making progress?"

"We think the scoring tool was trained on biased historical data," Amira said. "Which would mean it was already set up to favour the same projects and areas that were funded before."

Mrs Okafor looked at the diagrams on the table. She didn't say anything immediately, which Amira had learned was actually a sign that she was taking something seriously.

"Can you prove it?" she said finally.

"Not yet," Amira said. "We need the real data. Past winners. Application numbers by area. The criteria the tool used."

"Some of that will be in the public records," Mrs Okafor said. "The trust publishes an annual report. I'll find the last three."

She left. They opened the biscuits.

"Step one," Jay said, taking one, "understand how it works."

"Done," said Asha.

"Step two," Amira said, "look at the real pattern."

She turned to a fresh page in her notebook. At the top she wrote:

Chapter 2 of our investigation: the data.

CHAPTER 3

The Pattern Nobody Noticed

Mrs Okafor brought the annual reports on Thursday morning before the centre opened, leaving them in a brown envelope on the corner table with a Post-it note in her handwriting: *Don't lose these. Original copies.*

By the time the others arrived, Amira had already read through the first one.

"It's all here," she said, without looking up. "Every year. Every winner. Location, project type, score."

"They published the scores?" Jay said, dropping into his seat and pulling the laptop open.

"Partial scores. A summary range, not individual numbers. But enough."

Tomas picked up one of the reports and flicked to the awards section, running his finger down the page with the efficient focus of someone who'd once told Amira he'd spent a summer reading his older brother's business case studies for fun.

"Right," he said. "Let's build the picture."

They divided the work.

Amira tracked project types, dance, sport, technology, arts, cooking, debate, and noted which types had appeared most often in the winners list over six years.

Jay built a spreadsheet, entering each winner's name, area, project type, and score band.

Tomas cross-referenced the data against a borough map he'd pulled up on his phone, assigning each winning project to one of the four main areas of the borough: Riverside, Millbrook, West Side, and Eastside.

Asha handled what she called "the fairness wall", a growing grid of sticky notes on the window, colour-coded: yellow for Riverside, blue for Millbrook, green for West Side, pink for Eastside.

After forty minutes, Asha stepped back from the window and looked at her grid.

The window was almost entirely yellow and blue.

"In six years," Jay read from his spreadsheet, "Riverside received funding twenty-one times. Millbrook, seventeen times. West Side, nine times. Eastside..." He paused. "Four times."

"Four out of fifty-one awards," Amira said.

"That's less than eight percent," Tomas said immediately.

"While Riverside got over forty percent," Amira confirmed.

Jay leaned back in his chair and exhaled. "Okay. That's not subtle."

"But what does it mean?" Asha asked. She was still looking at the window. "Is Eastside just submitting worse applications?"

"Or fewer?" Tomas said.

"Or are they submitting good ones that keep getting rejected?"

"We don't know yet," Amira said. "This is correlation. It shows us a pattern, but it doesn't tell us the cause."

She'd learned the word correlation in a maths class last year and had been waiting for the right moment to use it. This felt exactly right.

"There's something else," Jay said, scrolling his spreadsheet. "Look at project types."

He turned the laptop to face the group.

In the winners' list, the most frequently funded project types were: performing arts, sport, heritage and culture, and debate or public speaking.

Technology projects had been funded twice in six years.

Community digital access projects: once.

"And those two tech projects," Amira said, looking at the page. "Which area were they from?"

Jay checked. "One Millbrook. One Riverside."

Silence.

"So technology projects from Eastside," Tomas said slowly, "have never been funded."

"Not once," Amira confirmed.

Asha peeled a fresh sticky note and pressed it to the centre of the window grid.

She wrote on it in capital letters: *PATTERN CONFIRMED.*

Then she peeled another and stuck it underneath: *But why?*

"The AI would have learned all of this," Jay said quietly. "Every single year of this data fed in. It would have learned that technology projects from Eastside don't win. So when ours came through"

"It scored us low before anyone even read our actual proposal," Asha said.

"Probably," Amira said. "We still need to confirm how the tool works. But yes. That's the shape of it."

Tomas had been quiet for several minutes, which usually meant he was building toward something. He looked at the sticky note grid, then at the spreadsheet, then at his phone screen where the borough map was still open.

"Here's what I keep thinking," he said. "This isn't just our project. This is every project from Eastside for the last six years. Every young person who applied and got knocked back, maybe didn't understand why, maybe thought their idea just wasn't good enough." He paused. "And it might have had nothing to do with their idea at all."

The room was very quiet.

"We need to know one more thing before we take this anywhere," Amira said. "We know the pattern. But we need to know whether the data is complete. Whether we're seeing the full picture."

"What do you mean?" Jay asked.

"The annual reports show us who won. They don't show us who *applied*. We don't know if fewer projects from Eastside applied, which would change the numbers, or if they applied in equal numbers and lost at the same rate."

"That's the missing data," Jay said, suddenly sitting forward, tapping his keyboard. "Of course. We're looking at output without knowing the input."

"Exactly." Amira wrote in her notebook: *Step 3, find application numbers.*

"Mrs Okafor might have those," Tomas said. "Or the trust's public records."

"I'll ask her," Amira said.

She stood, capped her pen, and looked at the sticky note grid on the window, all those yellow notes, all those blue ones, the thin scatter of pink in the corner.

"We're not finished yet," she said. "But we're getting closer."

CHAPTER 4

When Data Tells Half the Story

Mrs Okafor found the application numbers.

It took her two days of searching through old filing cabinets, but she arrived at the table on Saturday morning with a folder of photocopied records, not the full applications, which were confidential, but the intake logs: project name, submitting organisation, area, and date received for every application in the past four years.

"I couldn't find years one and two," she said. "The records from those years were kept by the trust, not us. You'd need to write to them directly."

"This is enough to start," Amira said.

Mrs Okafor looked at the wall of sticky notes, the spreadsheets, the diagrams. She stood there for a moment longer than usual.

"You've done a lot of work," she said.

"We have more to do," Amira said.

Mrs Okafor nodded, slowly, and left them to it.

Jay built the new spreadsheet fast, pulling the intake numbers across four years and sorting them by area.

The result was not what any of them expected.

"Eastside applied more than any other area," Jay said.

Everyone looked at the screen.

"In the last four years," he continued, reading carefully, "Eastside submitted thirty-one applications. Riverside submitted twenty-six. Millbrook, twenty-two. West Side, eighteen."

"So Eastside isn't under-applying," Asha said.

"No."

"They're applying more than anyone else."

"Yes."

"And winning less than anyone else."

"Four times out of thirty-one," Amira said. "That's roughly thirteen percent success rate."

"Riverside's success rate?" Tomas asked.

Jay ran the calculation. "Seventy-five percent."

Nobody spoke for a moment.

"That's not explainable by application quality alone," Tomas said. He was standing, which he tended to do when he was thinking through something large. "A difference of that size, between thirteen and seventy-five percent, isn't noise. It's structural."

"Structural," Asha repeated, writing it on a sticky note. "What does that mean exactly?"

"It means the problem isn't random," Amira said. "It's built into the system. The way the system is designed, or in this case, what it learned, produces the same unfair result every time, consistently, regardless of individual effort."

She paused, looking at her notebook.

"It means working harder doesn't fix it. Because the problem isn't the effort. It's the framework."

Asha stuck the sticky note on the window: *Structural = the problem is in the system, not the people.*

But then Jay found the gap.

He'd been running through the application records, cross-referencing area codes with project types, when he stopped typing mid-line.

"Hold on," he said.

"What?" Amira asked.

"These records, they're from the intake logs. Project name, area, date. But they don't include all the project information that was submitted. The actual application had a longer form. Community need section, project description, team experience, budget plan."

"Right," said Amira.

"The AI scoring tool would have processed the full application. But the data we have only shows us the summary." He looked up. "We're analysing the pattern of outcomes. But we can't see what the AI was actually given to score."

"Meaning?"

"Meaning we don't know what specific part of the application the AI was weighting highest. Was it the postcode? Was it the type of project? Was it the language used in the description? Was it the experience of the applicants?" He spread his hands. "We can see the shape of the bias. We can't see the mechanism yet."

"The missing data problem," Amira said.

"Yes."

"So even our analysis has a gap in it."

"Yes. We can say: there's a clear pattern of unfair outcomes. We can say: the AI system is likely repeating that pattern. But we can't yet say: *this specific thing* is causing it."

Tomas sat back down. "Does that matter for what we're trying to do?"

"It matters for credibility," Amira said. "If we present this to adults, to the trust, and they ask 'but what exactly in the scoring is unfair?' and we can't answer that precisely, they'll use the gap to avoid answering the bigger question."

"Classic deflection," Tomas said, with the resigned tone of someone who'd encountered it before.

"So we need to fill the gap," Jay said.

"Or get close enough to it," Amira said. "We might not be able to access the full application data. But we can do something else." She tapped her pen against the notebook. "We can talk to people who applied. Real applicants. From Eastside. And find out what their proposals actually contained."

"You want to interview them?" Asha said.

"Not formally. Just conversations. 'Tell me about your project. What was your idea? What did you put in the application?'"

"And then compare what they described against the scoring outcomes," Jay said, nodding. "See if strong proposals still got low scores."

"If they did," Amira said, "that tells us the scoring wasn't based on quality."

"And if a postcode kept coming up as the differentiating factor," Tomas added slowly, "that's something we could actually demonstrate."

Asha was already writing on a fresh sticky note: *Talk to real people. Data is not the whole story.*

She stuck it above the structural note on the window.

"Data is not the whole story," she read aloud. "But people are."

CHAPTER 5

Building Their Own Model

"If we're going to argue that the current scoring system is unfair," Tomas said on Monday afternoon, "we should be able to say what a *fair* system would look like."

"You want us to build one," Jay said.

"I want us to try. Not a real one, a model. A set of criteria that we think would score applications fairly. And then test it against the real data."

"If our model produces more balanced outcomes," Amira said, following the logic, "it supports our argument that fair design is possible. That the problem isn't inevitable."

"And it shows we're not just criticising," Tomas said. "We're offering something better."

Asha wrote on a sticky note: *Don't just point at the problem. Show the solution.* She stuck it to the top of the whiteboard before they'd even started.

They started by listing what they thought a grant for community youth projects should actually be measuring.

"Community need," Amira said immediately. "How much does the area actually need this project? You shouldn't be penalised for being in a deprived area, if anything, that should score higher."

Jay wrote it down. "How would you measure community need?"

"Deprivation index. Schools data. Access to existing provision, if there are already five dance academies in an area, a sixth one is less urgent than a technology club in a place where there are none."

"Project feasibility," Tomas added. "Can they actually deliver it? Do they have a reasonable plan? But you assess the plan itself, not assumptions about who wrote it."

"Team commitment," Asha said. "Have they shown they care about this? Are they embedded in the community?"

"That one's harder to score," Jay said.

"Why?"

"Because it's qualitative. It's not a number. You'd have to read what they wrote and make a judgement."

"That's fine," Amira said. "Some things require judgement. The problem isn't judgement, it's unexamined judgement. Judgement without awareness of bias."

They spent two hours on the model.

By the end, they had six criteria:

1. **Community need score**, based on public deprivation data for the project's area
2. **Gap in provision**, whether the project type was already well-served locally
3. **Project plan quality**, clarity, realism, specific goals
4. **Community rootedness**, evidence that the team was embedded in the community they were serving
5. **Reach and impact**, estimated number of people benefited
6. **Sustainability**, did the project have a plan beyond the grant funding?

They debated the weightings for longer than anything else. Tomas argued that community need and gap in provision should be weighted most heavily, "because that's the point of community funding." Jay argued that project plan quality needed to be high enough to avoid funding projects that wouldn't actually work. Asha kept pushing for community rootedness to matter more than it currently did on the whiteboard.

Amira listened to all of it, then said: "What's the current system's first criterion?"

They didn't know. That was the point.

Jay built it into a simple spreadsheet model and ran it against their reconstructed data, the summary information from the intake logs, supplemented by what they'd started to gather from applicant conversations.

The results were not a perfect inversion of the original system. But they were different.

Under their model, Eastside's average score rose by eighteen points. Riverside's average fell by eleven. The successful applicants were more spread across the borough.

"It's not perfect," Jay said, scanning the results. "There are some Eastside projects that would still score lower, because their plans weren't as strong, or their impact estimates were smaller. That's fair. That's how it should work."

"But the postcode isn't dragging them down anymore," Asha said.

"No. The postcode is essentially neutral. In some cases it's actually a mild positive, because the deprivation score helps."

Amira looked at the results for a long moment.

"We designed this in two hours," she said. "With no budget. No team of consultants. No grant funding of our own." She looked at the others. "And it's already more balanced.".

But Tomas had a question.

"We should run it blind," he said.

"What do you mean?" Jay asked.

"Remove the area names from the applications before scoring. So whoever, or whatever, is doing the scoring can't see the postcode or the area name. They just see the project."

"That's called blind review," Amira said. "It's used in academic publishing. Job applications sometimes."

"Does it actually help?" Asha asked.

"It removes one source of bias," Amira said. "It doesn't remove all of them. A well-written application from someone with access to writing support still has an advantage. But it's a meaningful step."

Jay added a note to the model: *Recommendation: anonymise location data at initial scoring stage.*

It was a small addition. One line. But Asha immediately stuck a note beside the whiteboard: *Small changes matter.*

They packed up as the centre began to close for the evening.

Jay saved the model. Amira photographed the whiteboard. Tomas transferred the recommendation notes into a document on his phone. Asha collected her sticky notes, peeling them carefully and re-sticking them in order on the front of her notebook so she wouldn't lose the sequence.

"We have a model," Jay said. "An alternative."

"We have evidence," Amira said. "A pattern, a gap, and a proposal."

"We still need the human part," Tomas said. "The conversations. The actual applicants."

"That's next," Amira said.

She closed her notebook and pulled her hoodie sleeves down over her hands, her thinking-finished gesture, Jay had noticed.

"We're building something real," she said. Not loudly. Just as a statement of fact.

Nobody disagreed.

CHAPTER 6

The Unexpected Consequence

It was Asha who found it.

She was running through the model results on Wednesday evening, checking that the criteria were applying consistently, when she frowned at the screen, that particular head-tilt that meant something wasn't sitting right.

"Jay," she said. "Can you check this column?"

Jay leaned over. "Which one?"

"Community rootedness. The scoring there, something's off."

He looked at the formula. It was pulling information from the application descriptions: years of operation, number of local volunteers, community partnerships listed. Simple enough.

But when he filtered by project type, a pattern emerged.

New projects, organisations that had only recently formed, were scoring very low on community rootedness, almost by definition. They hadn't had time to build partnerships. They didn't have years of operation. They were new.

"That makes sense," Tomas said, reading over Jay's shoulder. "Newer organisations would naturally score lower on a history-based criterion."

"Right," Asha said. "But look at *which* projects are new."

She scrolled down.

The newest organisations in the data were disproportionately from Eastside.

"Oh," Jay said quietly.

They were all quiet for a moment.

"We made it worse," Asha said. Then she corrected herself: "We made it different. But we didn't fix it. We moved the bias."

"We didn't remove it," Amira said. Her voice was flat, not upset, exactly, but very still. "We just changed its shape."

"How?" Tomas asked.

"Eastside has fewer established organisations," Amira said. "Partly because funding has historically been harder to get. So newer organisations, which form when existing ones can't serve a need, are concentrated in Eastside. A criterion that rewards organisational history is going to disadvantage them, because their lack of history is itself a consequence of the original inequality."

Jay leaned back in his chair. "We designed a criterion that sounds fair, who can argue against rewarding rootedness?, but which penalises exactly the communities that most need the funding."

"Because fairness isn't the same as neutrality," Amira said.

Asha pressed a sticky note to the window.

Fairness ≠ Neutrality.

She stared at it.

"So what do we do?" Jay asked.

"We fix it," Amira said. "That's what you do when you find a problem in your model. You don't pretend it isn't there. You redesign."

"How do you redesign community rootedness without penalising new organisations?" Tomas asked.

"You split the criterion," Amira said, picking up her pen now. "Instead of asking 'how long have you been operating?' you ask 'what evidence do you have of community connection?' Those aren't the same question. A group that formed six months ago can still have genuine community connection, they're just expressing it differently. Through founder backgrounds. Through who came to their first meeting. Through letters of support."

"Qualitative evidence instead of quantitative history," Jay said.

"Yes."

"That requires a human to read and assess it. You can't automate that as easily."

"Then maybe," Amira said carefully, "some parts of a fair system can't be fully automated. Maybe that's one of the things we say."

They spent another hour rebuilding the community rootedness criterion.

The new version asked three questions instead of assuming years equalled connection:

1. Who are the founders, and what is their relationship to the community they're serving?
2. What evidence exists that local people are involved in planning, not just benefiting?
3. What letters or statements of support have been provided?

"That's better," Asha said, running it through the model. "The Eastside new organisations score higher now. And some of the older Riverside organisations that were clearly serving communities quite different from their own... score a bit lower."

"Appropriately lower," Tomas said.

"Yes. Appropriately."

Jay was typing notes alongside the model. He wrote at the top of the document in bold:

Version 2, Revised after identifying unintended bias in original design.

He showed it to the others.

"That matters," Amira said. "That we're documenting what we found and what we changed. That's not failure. That's the process working."

"This is actually the most important thing we've learned," Amira said, as they wrapped up.

"What is?" Tomas asked.

"That you can try to build something fair and still get it wrong. Not because you're bad at it. But because bias is layered. Fix one layer and sometimes another appears underneath." She looked at her notebook. "It doesn't mean you stop trying. It means you build in a way that allows you to keep checking."

"Like version numbers," Jay said.

"Exactly like version numbers. Fair systems need to be updated. They need to be reviewed. They need someone asking, every time: *who is this still not working for?*"

Asha wrote the question on a sticky note, *Who is this still not working for?*, and stuck it in the centre of the window, slightly above everything else. The question mark was big.

"We should put that in the checklist," she said.

"What checklist?" Jay asked.

"The one we're going to make," Asha said, with the certainty of someone who had already decided this. "When we're done. The AI Builders Code."

She said the name like she'd been carrying it around for a while, waiting for the right moment to put it down.

CHAPTER 7

Asking the Right Questions

Priya had applied for a grant two years ago for a project called **Eastside Reads**, a community reading programme for primary-age children whose parents worked long shifts and couldn't always do bedtime stories with them. Trained teenage volunteers would visit families in the evenings, read with younger children, and help build home reading habits.

The application had been rejected. No feedback given.

She was twenty-three now, still running a version of the project on a shoestring, using donated books and her own evenings. Mrs Okafor had connected her to the team.

"I spent about three weeks on that application," Priya said. She was sitting across from Amira and Asha in the quiet room off the main hall, hands wrapped around a mug of tea. "Researched the criteria. Showed the need, there's good data on literacy gaps in this borough, it's not hidden. Costed everything carefully. Had three teachers write supporting letters."

"What score did you receive?" Amira asked.

"They didn't tell us scores. Just said our application was unsuccessful and they hoped we'd apply in future rounds."

"Did you apply again?"

"No." Priya looked at her mug. "It takes a lot out of you. And I had no idea what to change because I had no idea what went wrong."

Asha, very gently, asked: "Do you think your proposal was a good one?"

Priya looked at her, slightly surprised, maybe, at the directness from someone so young. Then she smiled.

"I think it was a really good one," she said. "I think the kids in our area needed it. I think we had the right team. I think we could have delivered it." She paused. "I still think that. We're still doing it. Just without the resources we needed."

Amira wrote in her notebook. She wrote down the project name, the year, the criteria Priya had described meeting, the letters of support. She noted that Priya hadn't used jargon-heavy language in describing her proposal, she'd described a community need simply and clearly, in plain English.

She wondered if the AI had weighted academic or business-style language more highly without anyone deciding it should.

She wrote: *Language register, possible bias vector. Check.*

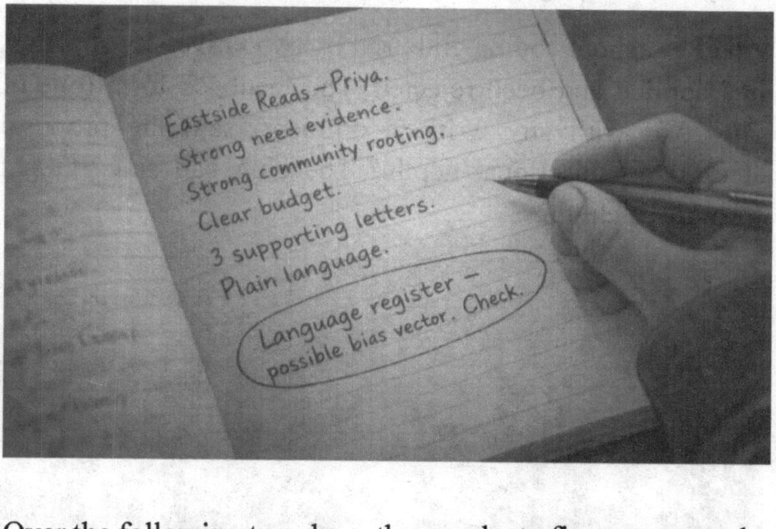

Over the following two days, they spoke to five more people.

Marcus, eighteen, had applied for funding for a youth boxing gym, not for competition, but as a structured after-school environment for young people who had nowhere safe to go between three and six pm. Rejected.

Fatima, thirty-one, had applied for a women's digital skills workshop, specifically aimed at older women in the Bengali community who had been excluded from technology adoption. Rejected.

Kwame, sixteen, had applied, with his teacher's help, for a community podcast series documenting the oral histories of elderly Eastside residents. Rejected. "They said it lacked scalability," he said. "I didn't know what scalability meant. I had to look it up."

A youth football team had applied for basic equipment, cones, bibs, a net. Small budget. Clear need. Rejected. They'd since bought the equipment with car boot sale money.

An after-school coding club, run by two university students, had applied and been rejected. The feedback form (one of only two with any written comment) said the proposal "lacked organisational depth." The club had since taught forty-three children.

Tomas had built a comparison grid.

For each rejected Eastside application, he'd noted: the community need level, the quality of supporting evidence, the volunteer or team experience, and whether the project had subsequently succeeded on its own, which most of them had.

The picture was consistent.

"These are good projects," he said. "Several of them are provably good, they've gone on to succeed without the funding. The need was real. The teams were committed. The plans were reasonable."

"And all from Eastside," Jay said.

"All from Eastside. All rejected. Several with no feedback. A couple with vague feedback that didn't correspond to any obvious weakness in what they described to us."

Amira looked at the grid.

"The data pattern, the model testing, and now the lived experience," she said quietly. "Three different types of evidence. They all point the same way."

"There's one more thing I want to ask," Asha said.

She'd been quieter than usual over the interview sessions, less sticky notes, more listening. They'd all noticed, but none of them had pushed.

"None of the people we spoke to felt like they'd been treated fairly," she said. "But none of them were angry at a machine. Because they didn't know there was a machine involved. They thought a human had read their work and decided it wasn't good enough." She paused. "Kwame spent hours on that application. He thought a person looked at it and said no. He didn't know an algorithm might have filtered it before a person ever saw it."

"That's a transparency problem," Amira said.

"It's also a dignity problem," Asha said. "If a machine is making decisions about people, or heavily influencing those decisions, those people deserve to know. They deserve to be able to question it."

She picked up her pen and wrote on a sticky note, slowly, more carefully than usual.

People have the right to know when AI is involved in decisions about them.

She looked at it for a moment, then said: "That's going in the code."

CHAPTER 8

The Fairness Checklist

"Let's write it properly," Amira said.

It was Saturday morning, a week and a half since the list had appeared on the wall. Outside, East London was doing what it always did: getting on with things, loudly, without particular concern for who was watching.

Inside, at the corner table with the wonky leg, four young people were building a document.

They called it the **AI Builders Code**, Asha's name, which had stuck without anyone formally agreeing to it.

"It should be practical," Tomas said. "Not just principles. Actual questions. Things a builder can check."

"Things a *community* can check," Asha added. "Not just the person who built the system. The people it affects."

"Both," Amira said.

They began.

The code took shape over two hours, with arguments and revisions and Tomas twice asking Jay to read back what they had so he could check it made sense from the outside.

THE AI BUILDERS CODE

A checklist for anyone building or using AI systems that affect people

1. Know your training data.
What examples did your AI learn from? Were those examples fair? Who was overrepresented? Who was missing?

2. Check for historical bias.
Does your training data reflect a past that was unfair? If so,

your AI may be learning to repeat it. Audit the outcomes your system was trained on before you trust its judgements.

3. Test your outputs by group.
After your system runs, sort the results by community, area, background, or other relevant categories. Are the outcomes equally distributed? If not, investigate why.

4. Look for missing data.
What information are you *not* collecting? Sometimes what's absent shapes the outcome as much as what's present.

5. Separate what is measurable from what matters.
Not everything that can be scored should be the only thing scored. Include criteria that require human judgement, and train your human reviewers to be aware of their own biases too.

6. Test for unintended consequences.
A criterion that seems fair in isolation may disadvantage certain groups once applied. Test every criterion separately, then in combination. Ask: who does this accidentally penalise?

7. Be transparent.
Tell people when AI is involved in decisions about them. Explain what it scores and why. Allow people to question the result.

8. Give meaningful feedback.
If a system makes a negative decision about someone, they deserve to know the reason in terms they can understand and respond to.

9. Build in review.
No fair system stays fair without maintenance. Set regular checkpoints to ask: who is this still not working for?

10. Include the people most affected.
The best design for a community system involves that community. Don't build for people. Build with them.

"Ten," Jay said.

"Ten," Asha confirmed. She was reading it over, tapping each point.

"I want to make sure number seven is clear," Amira said, pointing at it. "The transparency one. It shouldn't just mean 'put a note on the website.' It means actually explaining, in plain language, what the AI did and how someone can challenge it."

"Kwame," Tomas said. They all knew what he meant.

"Yes. Kwame looked up the word 'scalability.' He shouldn't have needed to. The feedback should have been in his language."

Jay updated the wording.

"And number ten," Asha said. "I want it to be the last one because it's the most important. You can follow one through nine and still miss the point if you didn't involve the community from the start."

"Agreed," Tomas said.

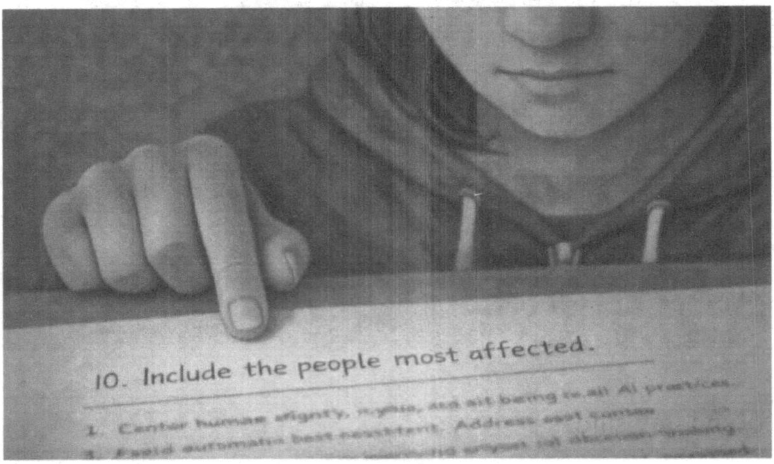

When the code was finished, they read it back in full.

Jay read it aloud, slowly, and the room was quiet while he did.

When he finished, Tomas said: "If the trust had followed this, even half of it, our application might have been treated differently. And Eastside Reads. And Kwame's podcast. And the boxing gym."

"Maybe," Amira said. "Maybe not all of them. Some might genuinely have had areas to strengthen. But they'd have had fair consideration. And they'd have known why."

"That's what this is about," Asha said. "Not that everyone wins. That the process is one people can trust."

She pressed a final sticky note to the top of the A3 sheet, not a new thought this time, but the oldest one, the one from the first day.

Fair for who?

"For everyone," she said. "That's the answer."

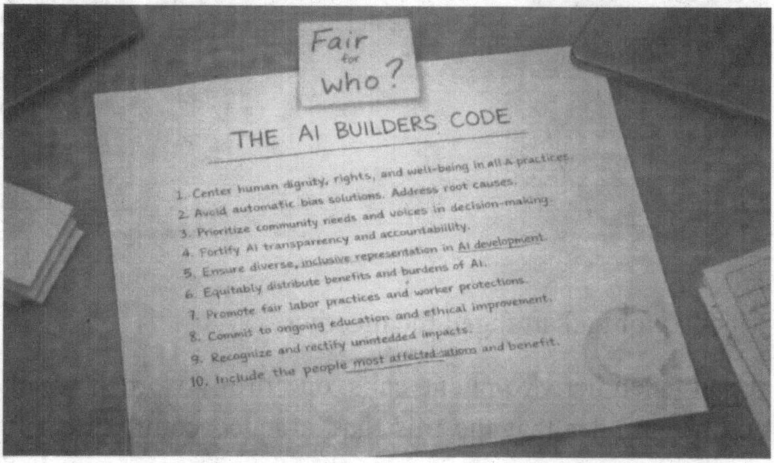

CHAPTER 9

Presentation Day

Mrs Okafor had arranged the meeting.

It had taken her two phone calls, one firmly worded email, and a reminder that the trust had a stated commitment to community engagement and youth voice. The response had been cautious but open: *We'd be happy to hear from them.*

On the morning of the presentation, they met at the youth centre first.

Amira was already there. She'd been there for twenty minutes.

"Ready?" Tomas asked.

"Yes," she said.

"Nervous?"

A pause.

"Nervous and ready are not mutually exclusive," she said.

Tomas smiled his sideways smile. "Fair enough."

Amira presented the data.

She didn't accuse. She didn't perform outrage. She stood at the end of the table and walked through what they'd found, point by point, in the same measured voice she used for everything.

The pattern of outcomes over six years.

The success rate discrepancy by area.

The application volume data showing Eastside applied *more*, not less.

The AI scoring tool and its likely training data.

The simulation Jay had run, demonstrating how historical bias replicates.

The interviews with rejected applicants, five voices, described carefully, with their permission.

The unintended consequence in their own model, and how they'd corrected it.

She spoke for twelve minutes.

When she finished, Jay presented the model. Tomas presented the recommendations. Asha presented the AI Builders Code, standing, reading each point clearly, making brief eye contact with each adult in the room.

When she reached point seven, *Be transparent*, she said: "The people we interviewed didn't know AI was involved in the decision about their application. They thought a person read their work. They blamed themselves. One of them, a sixteen-year-old, spent time looking up a word he didn't understand in the feedback, because he thought it described something wrong with *him*. It described something wrong with the process."

The room was quiet.

The grant manager, a woman in her forties named Helen, had stopped writing and was looking at Asha directly.

"How long have you been working on this?" she asked.

"About two weeks," Asha said.

Helen looked at the AI Builders Code document in front of her.

"This is rigorous," she said. Not warmly, exactly. But honestly.

Then came the harder part.

One of the trustees, older, wearing a tie, whose name was Richard, said: "I appreciate the work here. I do. But I think you may be drawing conclusions that go further than your evidence supports. You've shown a pattern of outcomes. You haven't proven a causal link between the AI tool and those outcomes."

Amira nodded. She'd expected this.

"You're right," she said. "We can't prove causation with the data we have. We'd need access to the full scoring records, which we've requested and haven't received." She looked at him steadily. "But the pattern is consistent, the statistical gap is significant, and the people affected deserve an explanation. The burden shouldn't be on them to prove they were treated unfairly. The burden should be on the system to demonstrate that it was fair."

Richard opened his mouth. Closed it again.

Tomas added, quietly: "You also have a public commitment to equitable grant-making. Equity doesn't mean everyone gets the same score. It means the process doesn't systematically disadvantage people based on where they live. The current data suggests it might be doing exactly that."

He didn't say it combatively. He said it as a statement of fact. Which made it harder to argue with.

Helen set down her pen.

"We will review the scoring tool's training data," she said. "We will request an independent audit of the last three years' results by area. We will consult with applicants from under-represented areas before the next grant round. And-" she held up the AI Builders Code, "-I'd like to formally propose that we develop this into a set of operating principles for our assessment process. With your involvement."

Amira looked at Tomas. He raised an eyebrow, impressed, or satisfied, or both.

Asha, very carefully, did not squeal.

"We'd be glad to," Amira said.

CHAPTER 10

Rewriting the Rules

Six weeks after Presentation Day, three things happened.

The first was that the Community Futures Trust published a public statement acknowledging "inconsistencies in the geographic distribution of awards" and announcing

Three announcements:

1. The trust would pause the AI scoring tool pending a full audit of its training data and weighting criteria.

2. They would re-open the most recent round for supplemental funding, specifically inviting re-applications from Eastside projects that had been strong on community need but scored low on historical organisational metrics.

3. The Eastside Digital Explorers Club would receive provisional funding to establish a permanent programme teaching AI literacy and ethical technology use to young people across the borough.

Mrs Okafor read the email aloud to them at the wonky table, her voice careful and professional, though Amira noticed her hand was shaking slightly when she set the phone down.

"Provisional," Tomas noted.

"Everything is provisional at first," Mrs Okafor said. "Until you prove it works."

"We can prove it works," Asha said.

They called it the **AI Builders Club**, dropping the "Digital Explorers" because this was bigger than exploring now. This was building. Carefully, thoughtfully, together.

The launch was a Thursday evening, six weeks after the presentation. The trust had provided five laptops, new ones, fast ones, that didn't wheeze when you opened more than two tabs. They'd also funded a second-hand projector, a whiteboard on wheels, and a modest budget for refreshments that Asha immediately organised into a colour-coded spreadsheet.

People came.

Not just the four of them. Priya came, bringing three teenagers from her reading programme who wanted to learn how algorithms worked so they wouldn't be scared of them. Kwame came, sixteen now, with a notebook full of ideas for a community podcast about technology and ethics. Marcus from the boxing gym brought two of his young coaches, lean and alert, who listened more than they spoke but asked sharp questions when they did.

Mrs Okafor had printed the AI Builders Code in large format and stuck it to the wall beside the window with the sticky notes, which Asha had carefully preserved, arranging them into a permanent display under a sheet of clear plastic.

Fair for who? was centred at the top, larger than the rest.

Jay ran the first session.

He stood at the whiteboard, marker in hand, and explained training data again, but this time to a room of fifteen people, ages eleven to twenty-four, from three different parts of the borough.

"Everything an AI knows, it learns from examples," he said. "So who chooses the examples? That's power. That's the moment where fairness lives or dies."

He drew the funnel diagram on the whiteboard, the same one from that first afternoon, but neater now, practiced. A girl in the front row, Priya's recruit, named Leila, raised her hand.

"So if the examples are wrong, the AI is wrong?"

"Exactly. And it's not because the AI is bad. It's because the AI is loyal. It learns exactly what you show it. Including your mistakes. Including your assumptions."

"How do you fix it?" Leila asked.

Jay grinned, that full, open grin that meant he was about to say something important.

"You keep checking. You keep asking who is missing. You build version two, version three, version ten. You never assume you're finished."

Tomas handled the external relationships.

He met with Helen from the trust once a month, presenting the club's progress, negotiating for continued funding, translating between the youth centre's informal energy and the trust's formal reporting requirements.

He was good at it. Better than he expected.

"I used to think I had to choose," he told Amira one evening, as they were packing up after a session. "Between the business side and the people side. Like they were different worlds."

"And now?" Amira asked.

"Now I think they're the same world. Business is just people moving resources around. If you forget the people, the business fails. If you remember them..." He shrugged. "You can do fair deals."

Amira wrote it in her notebook: *Tomas, integration. Standing between worlds as a bridge, not a barrier.*

Asha became the club's memory.

She kept the sticky notes updated, creating new ones for every session, every insight, every question that couldn't yet be answered. She developed a system, yellow for facts, pink for questions, green for solutions, blue for warnings.

Blue for warnings became particularly important as they started building their own small models. She would stick blue notes to the sides of monitors: *Check your outputs by area. Look for missing data. Who is this still not working for?*

She also kept track of the people. When Kwame missed two sessions, she texted to check on him. When Leila's mother couldn't afford the bus fare to get her to the centre, Asha quietly organised a travel fund from the refreshment budget.

"You're not just the sticky note person," Jay told her once.

"I know," Asha said. "I'm the fairness person. The sticky notes are just how I remember."

Amira watched them all.

She took notes, she always took notes, but she also learned to put the notebook down sometimes. To listen without recording. To trust that her memory, like any model, could hold important things without writing them down.

She found she liked teaching. Not standing at the front like Jay, but sitting beside someone, pointing at their screen, asking the questions that unlocked their own thinking.

"Why did you choose that criterion?" she would ask.

And then: "What would happen if we tested it against last year's data?"

And finally: "Who might this leave out?"

She asked it of everyone, but most often of herself.

One evening, as the autumn was turning to winter and the youth centre was heating up against the dark outside, she sat at the wonky table alone for a moment. The others were packing away the laptops. The sticky notes glowed on the window. The AI Builders Code hung on the wall, printed now, framed, official.

She thought about the list on the wall. The yellow paper that had started everything. It was still there, she knew, pinned to the corkboard, now covered by newer notices, but still present. A historical document. Training data for what came next.

She had been angry, she realised. Not at the start, she had been curious at the start. But underneath the curiosity, there had been anger. The kind of anger that came from seeing something wrong and not knowing if anyone else saw it too.

Now the anger had transformed. It had become practice. It had become method. It had become the ten points on the wall and the questions in the room and the faces of the young people who were learning to ask better questions than she had ever thought to ask at their age.

The light caught her glasses. A reflection from the streetlamp outside, silver and brief.

She was not finished. None of them were. There would be version two, version three, version ten. But she was no longer alone with the pattern nobody noticed.

Everyone noticed now.

The final session of the first term was held on the last

Thursday before Christmas.

They had planned to run a simulation, a full grant-making exercise where the club would score fictional applications using their own criteria, then analyse the results for bias. But instead, they talked.

Kwame, who had been granted the supplemental funding for his podcast, played them a clip, an interview with his grandmother talking about moving to East London in the 1960s, about the community that formed, about what it meant to belong somewhere.

"She's my training data," Kwame joked, and everyone laughed, but it was true.

Priya announced that Eastside Reads had received the funding they needed to hire a part-time coordinator. It wasn't much, but it was enough. Three of the teenagers in the room had already volunteered to be readers.

Marcus spoke about the boxing gym, not as a pitch for funding but as a story, about the young people who came through the door angry and left focused, about how structure and safety were forms of love.

"We need to build systems that see that," he said. "That see the value in things that aren't easy to score."

Asha wrote it on a sticky note: *Value isn't always easy to score.* She stuck it to the window, over the grid, where the light would catch it every morning.

At the end, Amira stood up.

She didn't have notes. She didn't need them.

"We started with a question," she said. "Fair for who?"

The room was quiet.

"We found that the answer was changing. It changed as we learned more. It changed as we built models and found their flaws. It changed as we met each other." She looked around the circle, at Jay, at Tomas, at Asha, at Kwame and Priya and Marcus and Leila and all the others. "Fairness isn't a destination. It's not a score you achieve and then stop. It's a practice. A question you keep asking."

She paused.

"The AI Builders Club exists because a system made a decision, and we asked why. We got some answers. We changed some things. But the work doesn't end. Next year, there will be new technology. New decisions. New patterns that nobody has noticed yet."

She smiled, a real smile, small but present.

"And we'll be here. Asking questions. Building version two. Version three. As long as it takes."

Afterward, they locked up the centre together, Mrs Okafor handing Asha the keys, trust established, passed on.

Outside, East London was cold and bright, the streetlights reflecting off wet pavement. The four of them stood on the step for a moment, not ready to split apart yet, their breath visible in the dark air.

"Book 2?" Jay asked.

"What?"

"There's Book 2, right? Fairness in... I don't know. Facial recognition? Hiring algorithms? There are other systems."

"Predictive policing," Tomas said quietly.

"School admissions," Asha added.

"Medical AI," Amira said. "Who gets treatment, who gets prioritised. All of it."

"So Book 2," Jay said.

"So Book 2," Amira agreed.

They walked down the street together, four figures in the winter dark, passing under streetlights that cast their shadows long and then short and then long again. Behind them, the youth centre glowed warm against the night, the sticky notes visible through the window like a constellation.

Fair for who?

The question glowed yellow against the glass, visible to anyone passing by, an invitation to look closer, to ask more, to build better.

They would be back tomorrow. For now, they walked home, notebooks under arms, minds full of version numbers, ready for whatever came next.

QUESTIONS FOR READERS AND CLASSROOMS

Use these prompts for group discussion, journaling, or project work after reading *The Bias Detectives*.

About Fairness and Rules

1. In Chapter 1, the list on the wall *feels* unfair before anyone proves it. How do you usually tell when something isn't fair, even without data?
2. Is a decision still unfair if nobody meant to be unfair? Why or why not?
3. Think of a rule at school or in your community. Who does it help most? Who might it accidentally make things harder for?

About Data and Patterns

4. Amira and her friends find patterns in who gets grants. What's the difference between noticing a pattern and jumping to a conclusion?
5. If you could look at data about one system in your life (school rewards, detentions, sports selections, etc.), what would you choose and why?
6. What kind of information might be *missing* from that data that would change how you understand it?

About AI and Responsibility

7. The trustees say the AI is just a "tool." Who do you think is responsible when a tool makes unfair decisions—programmers, users, organisations, or someone else?

8. Do you think there are some decisions that computers should never make about people? Give an example and explain your answer.

9. If you were building an AI for your school, what is one rule from the AI Builders Code you would insist on including first?

About Voice and Power

10. The applicants in Eastside never knew an AI was involved. How might the story be different if they had known from the start?

11. Have you ever felt like a decision about you was made "far away" by people who didn't know you? What would you have wanted those people to understand?

12. What can young people realistically do if they think a system (at school, online, or in their community) is unfair? Brainstorm at least three actions.

About Building Better Systems

13. The club's first "fair" model still had hidden bias. What does this teach us about making mistakes when we are trying to do the right thing?

14. Which question from the book do you think is most important: “Is it fair?”, “Who is missing?”, or “Who is this still not working for?” Defend your choice.
15. If your class started its own “Bias Detectives” club, what would be your first mystery to investigate?

About the Author

David King is a children's author and a doctoral researcher specialising in algorithmic bias and the social impact of artificial intelligence. His work explores how automated systems can quietly shape opportunities, choices and futures, and how we can design those systems to be fairer and more humane.

Before turning to fiction, David wrote *Legal and Humble AI*, which examined how law, ethics and computer science need to work together if AI is going to serve people rather than control them. His research and writing share the same goal: to make difficult technical ideas understandable, and to show that ordinary citizens, especially young people, have a voice in how technology is used.

David's vision is of a world where AI is built fairly, checked carefully, and used to help people achieve their potential rather than limit it. He believes that every algorithm should come with responsibility, that communities affected by AI deserve a say in how it works, and that asking "Is this fair?" is just as important as asking "Does this work?"

When he is not writing or researching, David enjoys visiting schools and libraries to talk with young readers about stories, science and justice. He hopes that *The Bias Detectives* will encourage a new generation to become builders, critics and caretakers of the technologies that shape their lives.

www.ingramcontent.com/pod-product-compliance
Lightning Source LLC
LaVergne TN
LVHW040515210926
848480LV00005BA/1474
9781909524392